A Gift For:

Miss Felishia

From:

Joshua R.

A Little Slice of Happy

Artist: Eric Disney
Writer: Cheryl Hawkinson
Designed by Chen Hsu

Printed and bound in China.

BOK5066

A Little Slice of Happy

ERiC

♥ ♥ ♥

Ahh, the first cup of the day.
Communing with your

coffee...
or tea...or cocoa.

The caffeine and you are one.

chat and a sip
with a friend.

A chance to **sit back
and catch up.**

A little oasis of pleasure.

Tea Time—a very civilized serving of *happy*.

In British mystery novels, the detectives can hardly solve a crime without a "cuppa."

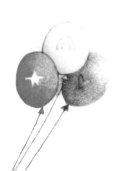

How delicious to savor
a favorite memory from the past.
It's like
experiencing
it all over again.
(Ask your endorphins.)

How wonderful to have
something to look forward to.
Even the word

"anticipation"

is fun to roll around
in your mouth.

Take any chance
to *Dance.*
...or prance, or wiggle and jiggle,
or jump up and down...even a birthday—
especially **your** *Birthday.*

FUN
FROCK!

HAPPY
WEAR

 chuckle a day
Keeps the **blahs** away.
And a full-blown giggle fit provides
a total body tune-up.

But a few moments of
soft **silence** is good, too.
Empty your mind,
then fill it up with
contentment.

Walking feels great...

...Walking and singing feels

FABULOUS!

Spend quality time
with a tree...
What better, more

solid *friend* could there be?

And a great listener...
not to mention back scratcher.

...Or find a garden.
Surround yourself with
flowers and something inside
you will bloom.

HAPPY
BOOT

Let's take a moment
to be thankful for shoes...
from the depths of our souls,
or soles, or whatever.
Once upon a time, shoes weren't
made for left and right feet—
you were stuck with the
same-shaped shoe for each foot.
Ouch. Life is **Good** now.

Oooh, the joys of the
luxurious soak.
Dissolve your troubles in bubbles.
Feel the stress float away.
Prepare yourself for
whatever **little surprise**
life brings you next.

Love a **little person.**
If you don't have a child in your life,
consider borrowing one.
Aunt-ing and uncle-ing
are noble professions.

It feels good to give—
to do a **little favor,**
to help someone out
at the last moment...
to be needed.

It's a gift to be
a gracious receiver, too,
to open your heart and take in the

Kindness that
comes your way.

nap with your cat
is always nice...

...or a snuggle with your dog.

Ummmmm, FOOD–
it's **satisfying** to make...

...delightful to share...

...and not
half bad
by itself...

...even on the *go.*

It's funny how sharing
something makes it
more satisfying, isn't it?

Whether it's shopping...

...or trying to
turn back
the clock.

Sometimes, you just want to
hang out with
a whole bunch of people...
get that group energy thing going.

You want to see
and be seen...

...and then go out for a

group snack!

Every day, celebrate a personal victory—
no matter how small.
You must have done
something to make yourself proud.
Go ahead—
shout out loud!

In fact, give yourself credit
for being you. Period.
Take a moment or two
to revel in your own

uniqueness.

You're one of a kind, Snowflake.

hy not let the child in you
come out to play?
Double dog dare ya.

Treat yourself to a little **adventure.** Do something that's totally new—for you.

Star light. Star bright.
     Look up at the sky tonight
and breathe in some of that

magical stardust.
     Don't worry—it won't
          make you sneeze.

A good book,
a cozy nook,
a sweet escape
into fantasy...

...perhaps a

late-night

rendezvous...

...and then those
blissful moments
just before you drift off
to Dream City—
that's one of life's biggest

Slices of Happy!

Cheryl Hawkinson didn't plan on being

a writer when she was growing up in Minneapolis, Minn.
She wandered around quite a bit before she found her way
to Hallmark, where she has been happily ensconced for
some time now, turning out a wide range of whimsy,
including the infamous greeting card, "He Was Only a
Chocolate Chip Cookie, but I Loved Him."

Eric Disney pretty much always liked to draw and hoped that one day he could actually make a living at it. Born and raised in Kentucky (Fort Thomas) and schooled in Ohio (Miami U), he eventually became an illustrator at Hallmark, where he is known not only for his quirky characters and distinctive color palette, but for his eclectic sock and tie collection.

If you have enjoyed this book,
or it has touched your life in some way,
Hallmark would love to
hear from you.
Please send your comments to:

Book Feedback,
2501 McGee, Mail Drop 489,
Kansas City, MO 64141-6580.
Or e-mail us at:
booknotes@hallmark.com.